HARRIET'S Ruffled FEATHERS

THE WOMAN WHO SAVED MILLIONS OF BIRDS

PICTURES BY
Romina
Galotta

JOY
McCullough

Atheneum Books for Young Readers
New York   London   Toronto   Sydney   New Delhi

ATHENEUM BOOKS FOR YOUNG READERS

An imprint of Simon & Schuster Children's Publishing Division

1230 Avenue of the Americas, New York, New York 10020

Text © 2022 by Joy McCullough

Illustration © 2022 by Romina Galotta

Book design by Greg Stadnyk © 2022 by Simon & Schuster, Inc.

For information about special discounts for bulk purchases, please contact

Simon & Schuster Special Sales at 1-866-506-1949 or business@simonandschuster.com.

The Simon & Schuster Speakers Bureau can bring authors to your live event.

For more information or to book an event, contact the Simon & Schuster Speakers Bureau at 1-866-248-3049

or visit our website at www.simonspeakers.com.

The text for this book was set in ITC Tiffany.

The illustrations for this book were rendered in watercolor.

Manufactured in China

1221 SCP

First Edition

2 4 6 8 10 9 7 5 3 1

Library of Congress Cataloging-in-Publication Data

Names: McCullough, Joy, author. | Galotta, Romina, illustrator.

Title: Harriet's ruffled feathers / Joy McCullough ; illustrated by Romina Galotta.

Description: First edition. | New York : Atheneum Books for Young Readers, 2022. |

Includes bibliographical references. | Audience: Ages 4 – 8. |

Summary: After learning about the millions of birds dying for their feathers, Harriet starts the Massachusetts Audubon Society,

dedicated to the conservation and protection of birds. Includes instructions on bird-watching and how to make pretend binoculars.

Identifiers: LCCN 2020041285 | ISBN 9781534486768 (hardcover) | ISBN 9781534486775 (eBook)

Subjects: LCSH: Hemenway, Harriet—Juvenile Fiction. | Massachusetts Audubon Society—Juvenile Fiction.

| CYAC: Hemenway Harriet—Fiction. | Massachusetts Audubon Society—Fiction. | Naturalists—Fiction. |

Birds—Protection—Fiction. | Conservation of natural resources—Fiction. | Fashion—Fiction.

Classification: LCC PZ7.1.M43412 Har 2022 | DDC [E]—dc23

LC record available at https://lccn.loc.gov/2020041285

For my mom
—J. M.

To all the trailblazing women who came before me
and the brave ones who will follow
—R. G.

Harriet loved a hat.
Wide-brimmed, bonnet, chapeau, straw.
Trilby, boater, flowerpot.

She loved hats with ribbons and flowers, embroidery and pearls. And feathers! What was better than a hat with grand, glorious feathers?

All the society ladies were wearing them.

One morning Harriet spotted a stunning
feathered bonnet in the *Boston Daily Globe*.
But it wasn't an advertisement for a new
milliner or a spread in the fashion section.

It was an alarming news story about the millions of birds who died so that Harriet and her friends could soar at the height of style.

Just then a blue jay perched outside Harriet's window, its spiky crest a stylish cap of its own. To think this bird should be deprived of its own finery for someone else's hat!

A passion for fashion was one thing, but this was featherbrained!

Harriet swooped across the street to where her cousin Minna sat having breakfast. "We must stop this senseless slaughter," Harriet announced.

"Certainly," Minna said. "Would you like a scone?"

Harriet loved a scone. But her feathers were too ruffled to eat!

Minna and Harriet agreed: They would no longer wear feathered fashions. But they were only two people. They'd have to do more if they were going to save the birds.

It was 1896. A new century was on the horizon, and change felt possible. Yet women didn't even have the right to vote. What could two society ladies do about a great big ostrich of a problem?

*You are cordially invited
to a garden tea party
at the home of Harriet Lawrence Hemenway
at 11:00 a.m. on Saturday, April 3.
Join us for the event of the season!
Wear your best hat!*

They decided to have a tea
party with all their friends.
Harriet and Minna had
many, many friends.

The women showed up in fine feather, sporting spectacular hats with massive plumes. Bluebirds, woodpeckers, egrets, gulls. Herons, warblers, swallows, owls. One hat boasted an entire stuffed hummingbird!

Harriet gathered her flock, welcoming them to her home. And then she told them, "Did you know that every year, five million birds are killed in the name of fashion?"

Some women were scandalized that Harriet had
spoken of such an unladylike thing. But most were
horrified to learn of the problem.

Before they left, the women pledged they would never again wear hats with feathers.

Harriet started noticing the birds in her
own backyard: American robins tugging
worms from the dirt. Black-capped
chickadees storing seeds away for winter.
Canada geese in a perfect V formation,
seeking water that hadn't frozen over yet.

Seeing these beautiful creatures thriving in their natural habitats made her more determined than ever to protect them.

Harriet and Minna had more tea parties to spread the word. They gave out leaflets explaining the cause. More than nine hundred Boston women joined their boycott of feathered hats.

They set up lectures with bird scientists to help people understand how to better protect our feathered friends. Hoping to form an organization devoted to the protection of birds, Harriet and Minna gathered powerful, influential people—doctors, professors, senators, and ministers. Together, they decided on the goals and methods for an organization.

Harriet and her fellow bird protectors became the Massachusetts Audubon Society, named for John James Audubon, an artist famous for his paintings of birds.

By the next year, there were 111 Audubon Society groups across the state.

Harriet and Minna weren't content to protect only the birds of Massachusetts. From the beginning, one of their goals was to encourage Audubon Society branches in other states. By 1898, more than ten states had their own societies.

These societies organized fundraisers, advocated for conservation laws, and even urged President Theodore Roosevelt to create federal bird reservations, where it was illegal to harm birds.

Across the ocean in England, Queen Victoria heard of Harriet and Minna's campaign and announced that she would never again wear a feather for fashion.

When the newly elected President Taft's wife, Nellie, wore a feathered hat to her husband's inauguration, Minna wrote her a strongly worded letter, explaining the problem with plumes.

The women used their knowledge and influence to get laws passed, making it illegal to buy or sell wild bird feathers. The Audubon Society grew into a national organization that still protects birds today, encouraging us to admire feathers exactly where they belong—on the birds in nature all around us!

Minna kept chirping until she was ninety-two years old. And Harriet twittered all the way to her one hundred and third birthday! Even when she was no spring chicken, Harriet loved to wander the woods, searching for birds and enjoying nature. She was known for her sensible walking shoes, and she always wore a hat.

Harriet loved a hat.

Author's Note

Several years ago, I learned about a young bird-watcher in England named Mya-Rose Craig. At the age of twelve, she had a birding column in her local newspaper. In 2020, at the age of eighteen, she was the youngest British person ever to receive an honorary doctorate in science, which was given to her by the University of Bristol. My interest in Mya-Rose led me to write a novel called *Across the Pond*, which is about a twelve-year-old girl who gets involved in bird-watching. And while researching that book, I learned about Harriet Lawrence Hemenway. I hope that learning about Harriet might lead you on an unexpected path of your own!

The National Audubon Society Today

More than a hundred years later, the group of bird conservationists started by Harriet Lawrence Hemenway and Minna B. Hall has grown into an organization that reaches millions of people each year. The National Audubon Society has more than four hundred local chapters across the country. They work with lawmakers and local officials to create conservation laws and protected habitats for wildlife, and to restore important ecosystems. They educate schoolchildren, their families, and all nature lovers about the natural world around them. They invite "community scientists"—bird-watchers like you, or like Harriet—to collect important information on the birds in their area, which helps scientists know how to help birds and wildlife.

The National Audubon Society has a lot of wonderful activities for kids and families on their website at https://www.audubon.org.

How to Bird-watch Like Harriet

The neat thing about bird-watching is that you don't need any fancy equipment or training. You can just step outside your house! Here are a few tips:

You'll find a lot of birds if you go to a forest or nature preserve. But you'll also find plenty in residential neighborhoods and city streets. If you're near water, like a lake or pond, you're going to find even more.

Birds are easier to hear than they are to spot. Close your eyes and listen for birdsong. Can you point in the direction the song is coming from?

Binoculars can be tricky to use, and heavy, too. You can enjoy bird-watching with just your eyes and ears. Or, for fun, make your own pretend binoculars! (See instructions on the next page.)

Make a game of it! Work together (or have a competition) to find a specific number of different kinds of birds, or try to find birds in as many colors as you can.

Imitate the birdcalls you hear. The more time you spend in the birds' backyard, the more you'll learn to identify different birds by their specific songs.

Finally, the most important thing is to enjoy the natural world! The goal isn't to learn the specific names of different birds or to see more birds than anyone else. It's to feel connected to nature and to your role in the natural world.

How to Make Your Own (Pretend) Binoculars

<u>Materials:</u>
2 cardboard rolls from toilet paper or 1 paper towel roll
colored or white paper
tape or glue
hole punch
piece of string long enough to go over your head like a necklace
markers, stickers, or other materials for decorating

1. If you're using a paper towel roll, carefully cut it in half (or have a grown-up help).
2. Set two toilet paper rolls, or both halves of the paper towel roll, side by side. Connect with glue or tape. If you've used glue, let the glue dry.
3. Decorate paper for the outside of your binoculars. You can color white paper or use colored paper or decorate with stickers—it's up to you. Wrap this decorative paper around the joined rolls and tape closed.
4. Use your hole punch to punch a hole on the outside edge of each roll, a half inch from the top.
5. Thread one end of your piece of string through the first hole, and tie a knot. Then thread the other end of the string through the second hole, and tie a knot there too.
6. Go bird-watching!

How to Be a Conservationist

A conservationist works to protect and preserve the environment and wildlife. You don't need a fancy degree or title to be a conservationist. Harriet was a conservationist, and you can be too.

When you encourage your family and friends to bike instead of drive, to cut down on water and electricity use, or to recycle, you're helping the planet. You can also encourage your family to use nontoxic cleaning products, since anything that goes down the drain ends up in the environment and can impact animals.

You can grow flowers and other plants that provide food for bees, butterflies, and birds. Set up a bird feeder, especially in the winter when food for birds is scarce. Pick up litter! And if you get to choose a topic for a school project, pick a conservation issue and spread the word to your classmates.

You can also be a citizen scientist by reporting your sightings of birds and other wildlife. Journey North has a website where you can learn about migrating animals, like hummingbirds and monarch butterflies, and record your sightings: https://journeynorth.org

The Center for Biological Diversity offers a list of things you can do as a kid conservationist to help protect and preserve the planet. You can find it here: https://www.biologicaldiversity.org

Bibliography

Mitchell, John H. "The Mothers of Conservation." *Sanctuary: The Journal of the Massachusetts Audubon Society* (February 1996): 1–20.

Packard, Winthrop. "The Story of the Audubon Society: Twenty-Five Years of Active and Effective Work for the Preservation of Wild Birdlife." *Bulletin of the Massachusetts Audubon Society for the Protection of Birds* (December 1921): 2–8.

https://www.masshist.org/news/story.php?entry_id=846

https://www.massaudubon.org/about-us/history

https://americacomesalive.com/2014/04/08/harriet-lawrence-hemenway-1858-1960-saving-birds-one-hat-at-a-time

https://www.smithsonianmag.com/science-nature/how-two-women-ended-the-deadly-feather-trade-23187277

https://davesgarden.com/guides/articles/harriet-hemenway-and-the-aububon-society

https://www.fws.gov/birds/news/200306harriethemenway.php